INSIDE COLLEGE FOOTBALL

MICHIGAN WOLVERINES

BY TODD RYAN

SportsZone

abdobooks.com

Published by Abdo Publishing, a division of ABDO, PO Box 398166, Minneapolis, Minnesota 55439.

Printed in the United States of America, North Mankato, Minnesota
022020
012021

THIS BOOK CONTAINS RECYCLED MATERIALS

Cover Photo: Lon Horwedel/Icon Sportswire/AP Images
Interior Photos: Tony Ding/AP Images, 5; Michael Young/AP Images, 6; Carlos Osorio/AP Images, 9, 27, 39; National Photo Company Collection/Library of Congress, 11; Bettmann/Getty Images, 15; AP Images, 17, 19, 21, 22, 25, 28, 30, 43; Tom DiPace/AP Images, 33; Albert Dickson/Sporting News/Getty Images, 35; Mark J. Terrill/AP Images, 36; Charlie Neibergall/AP Images, 40

Editor: Patrick Donnelly
Series Designer: Nikki Nordby

Library of Congress Control Number: 2019954414

Publisher's Cataloging-in-Publication Data

Names: Ryan, Todd, author.
Title: Michigan Wolverines / by Todd Ryan
Description: Minneapolis, Minnesota : Abdo Publishing, 2021 | Series: Inside college football | Includes online resources and index.
Identifiers: ISBN 9781532192449 (lib. bdg.) | ISBN 9781098210342 (ebook)
Subjects: LCSH: Michigan Wolverines (Football team)--Juvenile literature. | Universities and colleges--Athletics--Juvenile literature. | American football--Juvenile literature. | College sports--United States--History--Juvenile literature.
Classification: DDC 796.33263--dc23

TABLE OF CONTENTS

CHAPTER 1

BIG GAME IN THE BIG HOUSE

Excitement filled the air in Ann Arbor, Michigan, on September 10, 2011. For the first time in the University of Michigan Wolverines' 131-year football history, the lights were on in "the Big House," the nickname for their massive football stadium. And not only was it the first night game in the legendary stadium, but it was also a meeting with one of their fiercest rivals—the Notre Dame Fighting Irish.

The result was an unbelievable, heart-stopping experience. A record crowd of 114,804 filled the Big House. That is bigger than the population of many US cities. It didn't matter that neither program was at its historic best. A game between Michigan and Notre Dame was always a hot ticket.

Michigan's program was a storied success. The Wolverines had won 11 national championships and 42 conference titles to

Michigan wide receiver Jeremy Gallon runs downfield against Notre Dame in 2011.

10
adidas

The lights were turned on for Michigan Stadium's first night game when the Wolverines played Notre Dame in 2011.

that point. A losing season in the Big Ten Conference was rare for Michigan. After all, Michigan had more victories than anyone in college football. However, the Wolverines had losing seasons in 2008 and 2009 and were just 7–6 in 2010.

Like Michigan, Notre Dame was hoping to rebound after several subpar years. The Michigan–Notre Dame rivalry started in 1887. It had long been an important part of college football. Going into the 2011 game, Michigan led the series 22–15–1.

This game was also special because of the historic importance of the Big House lights. Ticket prices had jumped higher and higher, ranging from $185 to $600.

The famous stadium was built in 1927. Since then, all-time greats such as Tommy Harmon, Bennie Oosterbaan, Charles Woodson, and US President Gerald Ford had starred while wearing the Wolverines' colors—maize and blue.

As the players raced onto the Big House turf for the 2011 game, they were greeted by a "maize out," a sea of yellow shirts in the stands. The sound of "The Victors," Michigan's fight song, filled the stadium along with the cheers of pom-pom-waving fans.

But the joyful mood soon turned to despair. Michigan fell behind, and the Fighting Irish controlled the game. Notre Dame outgained Michigan 268–90 yards to take a 17–7 lead. The Irish had 15 first downs to the Wolverines' three. Notre Dame expanded its lead to 24–7 with 2:13 left in the third quarter.

HISTORIC HELMET

When coach Fritz Crisler introduced the unique "winged" helmet to Michigan in 1938, he wanted it to bring attention. And it did just that. The helmet was not only different but also had a practical advantage on the field, according to Crisler. He was convinced the bright yellow (maize) wing on a blue background would help Michigan's passers better see receivers downfield.

"There was a tendency to use different colored helmets just for receivers in those days," Crisler said, "but I always thought that would be as helpful for the defense as for the offense." Michigan made a successful debut wearing the new helmet when it opened the 1938 season with a 14–0 win over Michigan State.

There have been a few minor changes to the design over the years. And Michigan teams in other sports such as ice hockey, baseball, softball, field hockey, and even rowing later adopted the winged helmet.

BIG WINNERS

With an all-time record of 962–345–36 through 2019, Michigan had more wins than any other college football team, according to the National Collegiate Athletic Association (NCAA).

But Michigan fought back. The Wolverines scored two quick touchdowns early in the fourth quarter. Then junior quarterback Denard Robinson fired a 21-yard touchdown pass to junior wide receiver Vincent Smith. That gave Michigan its first lead of the night, 28–24, with 1:12 to go.

But the game was far from over. Notre Dame retook the lead, 31–28, on a 29-yard touchdown pass from Tommy Rees to Theo Riddick. Only 30 seconds remained. It seemed only a miracle could save the day for the Wolverines. Or a defensive blunder by the Irish. And that is just what happened.

Michigan sophomore wide receiver Jeremy Gallon was left uncovered by the Irish defenders. Robinson saw him wide open. Taking advantage, he fired a pass to his receiver. Gallon completed a 64-yard play before he stepped out of bounds.

Now the ball was on the Notre Dame 16-yard line with eight seconds left in the game. Michigan coach Brady Hoke had a choice. He could attempt a field goal that would send the game into overtime, or he could go for a touchdown to win the game. What would the Wolverines do?

Hoke went for the win. Roy Roundtree ran a pattern to the right side of the end zone. The team's leading receiver in 2010, Roundtree

× Michigan wide receiver Roy Roundtree scores the game-winning touchdown against Notre Dame in 2011.

was still looking for his first reception of the night. He battled for position in the end zone against a Notre Dame cornerback.

Roundtree jumped to catch the ball and landed with both feet in the end zone. The final score left Michigan on top 35–31. Robinson passed for 338 yards and four touchdowns, and he added another 108 yards and a touchdown rushing.

As Michigan's band played the school's fight song, fans stormed the field to celebrate. Players jumped into the stands, hugging other fans. It was undoubtedly an exciting finish. And in more than a century of football, the Wolverines had produced a number of them.

CHAPTER 2

A MICHIGAN MAN

"Hurry up, hurry up!" It was 1901—22 years after Michigan's first intercollegiate football game—and the school's new football coach, Fielding Yost, was driving his team hard.

Football then hardly resembled the game played today. It looked much more like rugby. And Yost's style was much different from the plodding way Michigan had traditionally played the game. Yost believed that a team with speed and agility could exhaust opponents. So he had the Wolverines play fast with groundbreaking offensive game plans. Yost's strategy featured the forward pass, which was foreign to most football teams at the time.

Yost had an unusual background when he applied for the coaching job at Michigan in 1901. He had spent one season each coaching Nebraska, Kansas, and Stanford. Michigan officials were impressed with Yost's demonstrated ability to quickly

Michigan coach Fielding Yost was renowned for building winning teams.

build a winning football program. So they hired him to coach the Wolverines. No one expected what happened next.

The Wolverines opened the 1901 season with a 50–0 victory over Albion and a 57–0 win over Case. Later in the season, the Wolverines posted a 128–0 victory over Buffalo. The Wolverines rang up 22 touchdowns in just 50 minutes of football in a game that ended early. After the first half, Buffalo's coach pleaded with Yost to shorten the second half to just 20 minutes. Seeing the pounding his Wolverines were putting on the opponent, Yost agreed.

Michigan was not only rolling up points at a rapid pace, but it was also not allowing its opponents to score. The Wolverines finished up the 1901 season without giving up a single point. Teams around the country were amazed. News of Michigan's awesome record started filtering in. The team had a 10–0 record and had outscored opponents 501–0.

Players in those days played both defense and offense. That season, Neil Snow was a fullback and defensive end for Michigan. He was captain of the team and an All-American. Snow had played one of his greatest games in the 1898 victory over Chicago that inspired Michigan's fight song, "The Victors." Another player, Harrison "Boss" Weeks, was an obvious leader. Yost moved him into the quarterback position. Halfback Willie Heston was another star. Heston's reflexes and strength were legendary. He finished with 72 career touchdowns.

Michigan's 1901 season was impressive. In four of the Wolverines' 10 games, the opposing team never had the ball in Michigan territory. Northwestern was the only team that got as far as Michigan's 35-yard line. The Wolverines' playmaking speed crippled opponents.

Michigan's next stop was the Rose Bowl. The Rose Bowl remains one of the most famous bowl games, and the Big Ten conference champion still plays there most years. Michigan played Stanford, the Pacific Coast champion, in the first-ever Rose Bowl that year. In the pregame parade, the Michigan players rode in a large carriage wearing maize and blue uniforms and waving colorful Wolverine banners. At Tournament Park, 8,500 spectators turned out to see the battle of football giants.

FIELDING YOST

During his 25 years as coach of Michigan football, Fielding Yost led the Wolverines to six national championships. It would be hard to top his first five years at the Wolverines' helm, in which he lost only one of 57 games. Later, as Michigan's athletic director, Yost was the driving force behind many new sports facilities on campus, including his pride and joy—the Big House, Michigan Stadium.

Playing under a blazing sun with temperatures in the mid-80s, Stanford made two goal-line stands. The California team turned Michigan away until late in the first half. Finally, Heston broke away for a 21-yard run to put the ball on Stanford's 8-yard line. Then Snow burst over the goal line for the first touchdown in Rose Bowl history. It started a landslide of points for Michigan. Snow added four more touchdowns in the second half. And Heston gained 170 yards rushing as the Wolverines buried Stanford 49–0.

With eight minutes still to play, Stanford captain Ralph Fisher walked over to the Michigan bench. He consulted with Wolverines captain Hugh White. "If you are willing, sir, we'll call it a day," Fisher said.

It had been a brutal contest. One Stanford lineman, a cousin of President Theodore Roosevelt, had suffered a broken leg. And he kept playing until he fractured three ribs. Stanford had no reserves left.

The Wolverines finished with an 11–0 record, outscoring their opponents 550–0. They were recognized as co-national champions along with Harvard. In those days, multiple teams could claim to be champion because different polls each named a winner.

In 1902 the Wolverines outscored their opponents 644–12 and won all 11 games for another national championship. Michigan again had unbeaten seasons and national titles in 1903, 1904, 1918, and 1923. The Wolverines became known as college football's "Point a Minute" team, and their coach was known as "Hurry Up" Yost.

Despite the numerous championships, it was a team that did not win the national championship that Yost considered his "best team ever." That was the 1925 squad featuring the great passing combination of Benny Friedman and Bennie Oosterbaan. Only a 3–2 loss to Northwestern in an unusually low-scoring game prevented Michigan from finishing with a perfect record.

Benny Friedman was one of the key players on Fielding Yost's "best team ever" in 1925.

Yost's retirement after the 1926 season did not signal the end of Michigan's success. Under coach Harry Kipke, Michigan won consecutive national titles in 1932 and 1933. And soon, a new player arrived to begin another dominant era in Ann Arbor.

CHAPTER 3

RUN FOR THE ROSES

There was no stopping Tom Harmon. It was the 1940 season, and the Michigan superstar halfback was running wild.

"Very seldom did one man tackle Tom," said teammate Forest Evashevski. "It took one man to slow him down, and then the others could pile on."

If they could catch him, that is. Harmon was known for awesome plays that left tacklers in the dust. One afternoon while facing Penn, he was trapped at the line of scrimmage. Harmon retreated 25 yards toward his own goal line. From one sideline to the other, he cut and twisted. Tacklers lunged at him. But he escaped. Finally, he broke free and headed out to the open field. Touchdown! Harmon had covered some 150 yards for that score.

Michigan standout halfback Tom Harmon turns the corner during a 1940 game.

MAD MAGICIANS

The 1947 Michigan team was known as the "Mad Magicians." Under Fritz Crisler, the Wolverines baffled opponents with a number of offensive formations. "Sometimes, watching from the side lines, even Coach Crisler isn't sure which Michigan man has the ball," reported *Time* magazine. As many as five players might handle the ball on one play. The sleight of hand in the backfield featured Bob Chappuis, Bump Elliott, Howard Yerges, and Jack Weisenburger. Together they worked magic, leading Michigan to an undefeated season and the national championship.

In 1940, the summer before his senior year, Harmon worked as a lifeguard. He had fun running up and down the sand for at least an hour a day, but he worked hard. He was in great shape for the start of the season. The Wolverines opened against the California Golden Bears on the West Coast. Instead of taking the train like usual, the Michigan football team flew to the West Coast. Today teams travel by plane all the time. But it was rare in 1940. The Wolverines became the first college football team to do so. It was exciting. Any team member under 21 had to get his parents' permission.

At the game, a surprise was being planned for Harmon. Evashevski waved away Harmon while he huddled with the rest of the team. Secretly, he told the team that it was Harmon's birthday. "Let's give him a present by everybody knocking somebody down." Harmon then took the opening kickoff 94 yards for a touchdown. His team had come through for him. The Wolverines went on to a 41–0 victory. "It was a firecracker start to a great year," Harmon said.

× Michigan halfback Tom Harmon, *center*, accepts his Heisman Trophy in 1940. Michigan coach Fritz Crisler looks on beside him.

Harmon's all-around performance against Ohio State in the last game of his college career helped him clinch the Heisman Trophy. Harmon did everything. He scored three touchdowns and passed for two more. He kicked four extra points, intercepted three passes, and punted for an average of 50 yards. A thunderous ovation from the opposing fans greeted Harmon as he left the field victorious. Michigan won 40–0.

During the early 1940s, World War II brought many changes to Ann Arbor. Michigan's campus was the site of a military officer training program. In the fall of 1943, more than 4,000 men in uniform were on campus. Among them were dozens of football players. Now playing for coach Fritz Crisler at Michigan was Elroy "Crazy Legs" Hirsch. He had been one of the country's top players at Wisconsin.

Hirsch made a bet he would score against his former teammates. As fate would have it, he was sitting on the sideline with a shoulder injury when Michigan played Wisconsin. But it was no matter. He

"AT ANY TIME"

The words "at any time" allowed modern-day football to develop. It was wartime in the 1940s. Many players went off to fight for their country. Michigan's football team was having difficulty filling its roster. Football at this time was an "iron man" game. The players remained on the field for the full 60 minutes. They played both offense and defense with no breaks. If a player left the game, he could not return in the same quarter. So before a game ended it was easy to run out of players.

Michigan coach Fritz Crisler asked for help. The NCAA approved a new rule. It permitted a substitute to enter the game "at any time." The free substitution rule allowed players to move freely in and out of the game. It was the beginning of two-platoon football, in which different players play offense and defense. Crisler became known as the "father of the two-platoon system."

Michigan back Bob Chappuis (49) fights off a tackler during the Rose Bowl against Southern California following the 1947 season.

had a solution. Into the game he went, and he kicked the final extra point. Hirsch won his bet, and Michigan won the game.

During the war years, players came and went. They had to leave school to go off to war. So finding experienced players became a problem for Michigan and Crisler. But then they all came back. In 1945 the war was over. Crisler had his pick of candidates. By that time, players were playing on one side of the ball, either offense or defense, not both.

Bob Chappuis was one of the players who returned to Michigan. The triple-threat back had played on a 7–3 Michigan team in 1942 before going off to war. Michigan now also had other talented players four and five deep at just about every position.

But none of them stood out like Chappuis. He was honored as the Wolverines' Most Valuable Player in 1946. The 1947 team featured the "dream" backfield of Chappuis, Chalmers "Bump" Elliott, Howard Yerges, and Jack Weisenburger.

✖ Michigan players carry head coach Bennie Oosterbaan off the field after he coached his final game in 1958.

By the time the regular season ended with a 21–0 victory over Ohio State, the Wolverines had carved out a 9–0 record. They were headed to the Rose Bowl. Their opponent was the University of Southern California (USC) Trojans. With Chappuis leading the way, the Wolverines produced a record 491 yards on offense. And they won 49–0. The score was identical to their first Rose Bowl after the 1901 season.

The Rose Bowl victory confirmed the top ranking for Michigan. Some were calling it the greatest Michigan team of all time. Another national championship followed. The 1948 team, under head coach and former All-America wide receiver Bennie Oosterbaan, was voted number one after a 9–0 season. All-America quarterback Pete Elliott led the Wolverines that season.

The 1950 season ended in another Rose Bowl appearance for the Wolverines. It was Oosterbaan's only visit to a bowl game during his 11 seasons at Michigan. In 1959 the Wolverines hired another former Michigan star to coach the team. Just 34 years old, Bump Elliott was the youngest coach in the Big Ten. He had a tough job. The Wolverines had only won two games in 1958. Elliott's first year as the Michigan coach was also a losing season.

Elliott felt it would take three to five years to rebuild and win a championship. He was wrong—it took six. In 1964 the Wolverines won nine games and finished first in the Big Ten. Then they routed Oregon State 34–7 in the Rose Bowl.

Elliott stepped down as coach following the 1968 season. It did not take Michigan long to find his replacement. And the new guy proved to be more than capable of continuing the Michigan tradition.

TOUGH SLEDDING

Amid blizzard conditions and winds swirling up to 28 miles per hour (45 km/h), Michigan beat Ohio State in their 1950 meeting known as the "Snow Bowl." Noted Michigan halfback Chuck Ortmann said, "You'd be running, and you'd have a little traction; all of a sudden you'd hit a frozen area. Your feet would go out from under you, and you'd fall down." Wolverines halfback Leo Koceski said, "It was cold, it was nasty, and it wasn't any fun." At least it was a victory, 9–3 in favor of Michigan.

CHAPTER 4

THE GREATEST RIVALRY

The story of Bo Schembechler and Woody Hayes began in Ohio, which is known as the Buckeye State. Schembechler played for Hayes at Miami of Ohio and then was his assistant at Ohio State. "Woody taught me more about the game than anyone could," Schembechler said. But Schembechler had to make a decision. After the 1968 season, Michigan—Ohio State's hated rival—offered him the position of head coach.

Hayes felt betrayed when Schembechler joined Michigan. After all, like Hayes, Schembechler had been born and raised a Buckeye. How could he go to the enemy? Hayes had once called Schembechler a friend. But that was no longer the case.

"It was a very personal rivalry," said Earle Bruce, who succeeded Hayes as coach at Ohio State. "And for the first and

Bo Schembechler turned the program around in a hurry after he took over in 1969.

only time, it was as much about the coaches as it was about the game."

A story about Hayes on a recruiting trip to Michigan is a good example of the rivalry. On the way home, his car ran out of gas near the Ohio border. Hayes and another coach got out and pushed the car over the border. Then they got gas. There was no way the state of Michigan was getting "a cent of my money," Hayes said.

For 10 years, the rivalry between Hayes and Schembechler continued. It became known as the "10-Year War." During that time,

LITTLE BROWN JUG

Michigan and Minnesota play for the Little Brown Jug. It is one of the most famous football trophies in the country. As the story goes, Michigan coach Fielding Yost carried the gray earthenware jug around with him so that his players could drink fresh Ann Arbor spring water. On a 1903 visit to Minneapolis, the Wolverines played to a 6–6 standstill with the Golden Gophers.

The embarrassed Michigan players, known for their powerful offense, were in such a hurry to get out of Minneapolis that they left the jug behind. A janitor found the jug while cleaning up the next morning. When Michigan inquired about the jug, Minnesota replied, "If you want it, come up and win it."

They have been fighting for it ever since. Today, the jug is painted half blue for Michigan and half maroon for Minnesota. The scores of each game in the rivalry are printed on it.

Michigan and Minnesota play each year for the rights to claim the famous Little Brown Jug.

from 1969 to 1978, the two coaching giants received as much or more media attention than their teams did every time they met.

The Michigan game was always the big one for Hayes, although he refused to say the name of the school. Hayes always referred to Michigan as "that school up north."

The record between the two schools was nearly even. Michigan and Schembechler held a 5–4–1 edge over Ohio State and Hayes. During their time, Michigan and Ohio State dominated the Big Ten. The rivals won all 10 conference titles in that span, and the other team finished second eight times. The Big Ten then was often

Michigan quarterback Don Moorhead runs with the ball against USC in the Rose Bowl on January 1, 1970.

referred to as "the Big 2 and Little 8." It was Michigan and Ohio State, and then everyone else.

Dozens of famous games had been featured in the rivalry. In 1968, one year before Schembechler took over, the Buckeyes had crushed the Wolverines 50–14 on the way to the national championship. Hayes took great delight in running up the score against Michigan. Near the end of that game, he ordered his team to go for two points after a touchdown. The Wolverines and their fans were steamed. When asked why he went for two points late in a game that was already decided, Hayes quipped: "Because I couldn't go for three."

One year later, the Buckeyes were going for their second straight national championship. One game remained on their schedule—Michigan. Schembechler, in his first year, had a plan. In practices leading up to the game, he had his players wear a tiny No. 50 on their jerseys. This was a reminder of the previous year's score, 50–14. *Be angry*, he told his players. *Do not let it happen again.*

Riding a 22-game winning streak, the Buckeyes were heavy favorites. Football experts were calling Ohio State unbeatable. But Schembechler did not appear to be concerned. He knew how he could beat his former boss. He had learned how from Hayes himself. Hayes had said to always attack an opponent at its strongest point. In this case, Michigan would attack Rex Kern, the Buckeyes' quarterback.

THE BIG HOUSE

Michigan Stadium is known as "the Big House." As of 2019, the stadium's official capacity was 107,601. That is quite a difference from Regents Field, where the Wolverines once played their home games. It originally seated 400. Growing interest in football forced the building of Ferry Field, which was opened in 1906. Its capacity eventually increased to 46,000. Fielding Yost made the push for a bigger stadium. Michigan Stadium was completed in 1927 at a cost of $950,000. The original seating capacity was 72,000.

✕ Schembechler, *left*, and Woody Hayes were key figures in the rivalry between Michigan and Ohio State.

"We didn't want Kern running the football," Schembechler said, "so we set our defenses to stop him."

The Buckeyes took an early 6–0 lead. Michigan came back to go ahead 7–6. Senior fullback Garvie Craw scored the first of his two touchdowns on a three-yard plunge. It was the first time Ohio State had trailed all year.

Kern then led the Buckeyes on a 74-yard touchdown drive. But Michigan again came back on Craw's one-yard touchdown run to go ahead 14–12.

Michigan quarterback Don Moorhead, meanwhile, was having a better day than Kern. He carried the ball for 68 yards, including a

DOMINANT RIVALS

Ohio State and Michigan have combined to win 80 Big Ten titles and 19 national championships through 2019. In addition, they have produced 10 Heisman Trophy winners and have had more than 60 players and coaches selected into the College Football Hall of Fame.

one-yard touchdown run to put the Wolverines up 21–12. Tim Killian added to the Michigan lead with a 25-yard field goal later in the second quarter.

It was becoming a tough day for Kern. Michigan's secondary picked off four of his passes. By the fourth quarter, Kern was so upset that he was forced to take a seat on the bench.

"The strategy was to contain Kern," Schembechler said. With 13 minutes left, the Buckeyes were on their own 42. They needed only one yard for a first down. Kern kept the ball and ran to his left, but he was tackled for a two-yard loss. The Wolverines took over the ball and went on to a 24–12 victory. Michigan had its revenge.

Hayes was upset. Not only did he hate losing to Michigan and his former assistant, but he lost a chance to compete for a second straight national championship. The Wolverines went on to the Rose Bowl instead. It was Schembechler's first of 10 appearances in the postseason bowl known as the "granddaddy of them all."

CHAPTER 5
BACK ON TOP

Bo Schembechler retired after the 1989 season. Gary Moeller took over and led Michigan to the Rose Bowl in his second and third seasons. But then the Wolverines began struggling. Starting in 1993, they had four consecutive seasons with four losses each. It was the worst four-year stretch for Michigan since the 1930s.

In 1996 Michigan finished seventh in the Big Ten in scoring and sixth in total offense. The outlook did not look any better going into the 1997 season. *Sports Illustrated* ranked the Wolverines number 18 in the country. They were just about ignored as a serious contender for the national championship.

Coach Lloyd Carr had taken over in 1995. He was looking for more offense. His star tailback, Tim Biakabutuka, had departed for the National Football League after that first season. One day before the 1997 season, Carr was leaving a dinner for recruits with Charles Woodson, his talented cornerback, when he had an idea.

Michigan wide receiver Desmond Howard makes a leaping touchdown catch in 1991.

HOWARD
21

HEISMAN POSE

Ohio State should have known better than to kick the ball to Desmond Howard, Michigan's great punt return man. But in the second quarter of their game in 1991, they did just that. It was a big mistake.

Taking the ball at the 7-yard line, Howard avoided three Buckeye defenders, scooted down the sideline, and streaked into the end zone. Howard then struck a Heisman Trophy pose after the school-record 93-yard punt return. The Heisman Trophy is given to the best football player in the country. It is a bronze statue of a football player sidestepping and straight-arming his way downfield to a mythical touchdown.

"Hello, Heisman!" exclaimed play-by-play announcer Keith Jackson. Hello, indeed. The runback helped clinch the Heisman Trophy for Howard, one of three won by Michigan players through the years. The others were Tom Harmon (1940) and Charles Woodson (1997). More recently, linebacker Jabrill Peppers was a finalist for the award in 2016.

"Charles," he asked, "how would you like to play some tailback?" Woodson thought about the abuse the position takes. "How about wide receiver?" Woodson countered.

It was the first day of practice. But with this new position added to his duties, Woodson put on an all-star show. Carr was delighted. He had found the offense he was looking for.

At first Woodson was not sure about playing on both offense and defense. But then he realized it gave him more opportunities to have an impact on the game.

Charles Woodson starred on defense, offense, and special teams for Michigan from 1995 to 1997.

Michigan opened the 1997 season with blowouts of Colorado and Baylor. By the time the Wolverines reached the final game of the regular season against Ohio State, they were 10–0. The Associated Press media poll ranked Michigan number one.

The Buckeyes were a tough opponent. They had lost only one game all year and were ranked number four. A record crowd of 106,982 at Michigan Stadium watched as Woodson put on an amazing performance. He set up Michigan's first touchdown with a 37-yard pass reception. Then he returned a punt 78 yards for a touchdown and intercepted a pass in the end zone. The Wolverines went on to a 20–14 victory.

Michigan cornerback Charles Woodson makes a midair interception against Washington State in the Rose Bowl after the 1997 season.

Woodson was now being considered for one of football's highest honors—the Heisman Trophy. When he was just a child, his dream was to win that award.

"That dream kind of left" when he became a defensive player, said Woodson. A player who spent most of his time on defense had not won the Heisman since it was established in 1935. Tennessee quarterback Peyton Manning was considered the likely Heisman winner in 1997. Instead, Woodson took home the award.

Woodson stepped up to the podium at the Downtown Athletic Club in New York with tears in his eyes and accepted the award. "My body just went limp, I couldn't really move," Woodson said. "I had to grasp what just happened."

It was Michigan's second Heisman in seven years, following Desmond Howard's win in 1991. Now it was time for the Rose Bowl and a meeting with the Washington State Cougars. A victory would give the Wolverines the national championship.

Woodson did not wait long to make his presence known. In the first quarter, he intercepted a pass by Washington State quarterback Ryan Leaf in the end zone. Late in the game, Michigan was clinging to a 21–16 lead. Washington State was on the move. The Cougars had the ball on Michigan's 26-yard line after a 26-yard gain. The clock was stopped momentarily to move the chains.

Two seconds remained. With no timeouts left, Leaf spiked the ball into the ground to stop the clock. But it was too late.

"THE VICTORS"

He never scored a touchdown, but Louis Elbel made one of the greatest contributions to Michigan football. He was in the stands on Thanksgiving Day in 1898 when Michigan beat Chicago 12–11. It ended a perfect season and gave the Wolverines their first Western Conference championship. The excited Elbel, a music student, wrote a fight song on the train back to Ann Arbor. In April 1899, the public heard the rousing song for the first time. Thus Michigan's famous fight song, "The Victors," was born.

The scoreboard clock at the top of the Rose Bowl stadium showed nothing but zeros.

The Washington State fans wanted to know what happened. They felt cheated. But when Leaf appealed to an official, the referee just shook his head.

Michigan quarterback Brian Griese was voted player of the game after passing for three touchdowns and 251 yards. Griese's father, a former all-pro quarterback, had performed on the very same field for Purdue.

The Wolverines and their fans celebrated their first national championship since 1948. Carr never approached another national title, although his run in 13 years in the Big Ten was largely successful. After 1997 his Michigan teams won four more conference championships. And the Wolverines played in a bowl game after each of Carr's seasons in Ann Arbor.

Michigan went into a slump after Rich Rodriguez took over as head coach in 2008. He was fired after three years. The Wolverines were a combined 15–22 under Rodriguez, and they never finished better than seventh in the Big Ten.

Brady Hoke replaced Rodriguez as the Michigan coach in 2011. Hoke focused on beating the team's biggest rival. He led the Wolverines to an 11–2 record, including a 40–34 win over Ohio State. Unfortunately, it was the only time Hoke beat Ohio State. And he didn't win enough games in general. Hoke was fired after a 5–7 season in 2014.

Michigan turned to former quarterback Jim Harbaugh to lead the Wolverines.

After two missteps at head coach, Michigan knew what it wanted: another Michigan Man. And it wanted someone who had experienced success. Former Wolverines quarterback Jim Harbaugh fit that bill. He had taken the San Francisco 49ers to the Super Bowl just a few years earlier.

Harbaugh was hired in December 2014. Fans were thrilled that a great Wolverines player who had become a great coach had come back to help his alma mater. But the Harbaugh era got off to a rocky start. The team lost his first game in charge to Utah.

Linebacker Jabrill Peppers continued Michigan's tradition of versatile athletes by helping out on offense and special teams in 2015 and 2016.

The Wolverines rebounded to post a 10–3 record. That included a rout of Florida in the Citrus Bowl. Harbaugh had Michigan in even better shape in 2016. The Wolverines were ranked third heading into the last game of the year with No. 2 Ohio State. It was a rivalry game with the added pressure of a College Football Playoff spot on the line. After years of deciding the national title by polls or computers, the CFP was introduced after the 2014 season, featuring the nation's four best teams.

Michigan held a late lead but allowed Ohio State to tie the game with a field goal as time expired. In double overtime, it looked like Michigan had the Buckeyes stopped on fourth down. But after a measurement, the Buckeyes were awarded a first down, and they scored on the next play to win the game.

MICHIGAN'S GREATEST

Jim Harbaugh was one of the finest quarterbacks in Michigan history. He was a Heisman Trophy finalist as a senior in 1986 as he led his team to the Rose Bowl. The Wolverines lost only three games with Harbaugh as a starter in his final two seasons. He left Ann Arbor as the all-time leader in passing yards with 5,449. Harbaugh was a first-round pick of the Chicago Bears in 1987 and started 140 games in a 14-year NFL career.

Harbaugh struggled to get Michigan back to playoff contention. The Wolverines rose to No. 4 in 2018, but their playoff hopes were again dashed by Ohio State. The Buckeyes routed Michigan 62–39. It was the most points Michigan had ever allowed to Ohio State.

The Wolverines were certainly a strong team under Harbaugh. They made bowl games and contended for Big Ten titles. But they still struggled to beat Ohio State and make the CFP. Michigan fans knew they had their coach in Harbaugh. They hoped he was the man to get them back in national title contention.

TIMELINE

1879

Michigan plays and wins its first intercollegiate football game on May 30 against Racine College in White Stocking Park in Chicago.

1901

Fielding Yost begins his long term of service as Michigan's football coach. The undefeated Wolverines claim the national title in his first season.

1902

Michigan appears in the first Rose Bowl on January 1, defeating Stanford by a score of 49–0.

1902

Michigan wins its second national title after an 11–0 season.

1904

Michigan wins its fourth straight national championship, sharing the honors with Penn of the Ivy League.

1918

Michigan and Pittsburgh are recognized as co-national champions.

1923

Michigan shares the top spot with Illinois as Yost wins his sixth and final national championship.

1927

Michigan Stadium opens on October 1.

1932

Coach Harry Kipke leads the Wolverines to the national championship, sharing the title with USC.

1940

Tom Harmon wins Michigan's first Heisman Trophy.

Fritz Crisler, who helped create the two-platoon system, leads the "Mad Magicians" to the national championship.

1947

Bennie Oosterbaan takes over for Crisler and promptly leads the Wolverines to a second straight championship.

1948

Michigan beats Ohio State 9–3 in the infamous "Snow Bowl" in Columbus, Ohio. Blizzard conditions prevail throughout, and teams are forced to punt a combined 45 times.

1950

Bo Schembechler takes over as the Wolverines' head coach.

1969

Schembechler passes Yost as Michigan's all-time leader in wins in a 26–24 win over Ohio State.

1986

Desmond Howard wins the Heisman Trophy.

1991

Under Lloyd Carr, the Wolverines win their first national title since 1948. Charles Woodson becomes the third Michigan player to win the Heisman.

1997

A 48–42 loss to Purdue assures Michigan of its first losing season in 41 years and ends the program's bowl streak at 33 years.

2008

Former quarterback Jim Harbaugh comes back to campus as head coach.

2015

Michigan wins a share of its first Big Ten East title but misses out on the Big Ten Championship Game by losing to Ohio State.

2018

QUICK STATS

PROGRAM INFO

University of Michigan
Wolverines (1879–)

NATIONAL CHAMPIONSHIPS

1901, 1902, 1903*, 1904*, 1918*, 1923*, 1932*, 1933, 1947, 1948, 1997*

OTHER ACHIEVEMENTS

Conference championships: 42
Division titles (2011–): 1
Bowl record: 21–27

KEY COACHES

Lloyd Carr (1995–2007)
122–40–0, 6–7 (bowl games)
Bo Schembechler (1969–89)
194–48–5, 5–12 (bowl games)
Fielding H. Yost (1901–26)
165–29–10, 1–0 (bowl games)

KEY PLAYERS

Anthony Carter (WR, 1979–82)
Bob Chappuis (HB, 1942, 1946–47)
Braylon Edwards (WR, 2001–04)
Benny Friedman (QB, 1924–26)
Tommy Harmon (HB, 1938–40)**
William Heston (HB, 1901–04)
Desmond Howard (WR/KR, 1989–91)**
Ron Johnson (HB, 1966–68)
Ron Kramer (E, 1954–56)
Jake Long (OL, 2004–07)
Bennie Oosterbaan (E, 1925–27)
Jabrill Peppers (LB/RB, 2014–16)
Denard Robinson (QB, 2009–12)
Charles Woodson (DB, 1995–97)**

HOME STADIUM

Michigan Stadium (1927–)

*Denotes shared title
** Heisman Trophy winner
All statistics through 2019 season

QUOTES AND ANECDOTES

Charles Gayley was a new student at Michigan in 1876. He had traveled in England and Ireland and loved rugby. He was happy to see that US students were playing a game similar to rugby called "foot-ball." But there was one problem: they were playing with too many players. He suggested rugby rules with one exception. Use only 11 players on each side, just the same as Harvard and Yale. With the new rules, the modern era of football was on its way.

Superstardom vs. education? Aaron Ward, a former Michigan hockey player, found out just where Bo Schembechler stood on the subject. Ward had been invited by the Michigan football coach to play in a golf tournament. "We had just won the Stanley Cup and it wasn't, 'Hey, Aaron, congratulations on the Stanley Cup.' He looked at me, plain as day, put his hand out and said, 'When are you going to finish your degree?'"

The Wolverines prepared for the Rose Bowl following the 1901 season in Waterman Gymnasium. The team did indoor work in the gymnasium and ran plays outside. Michigan coach Fielding Yost had an idea: build a facility with high ceilings and a dirt floor. The building could be used for practices. It was built 24 years later and called a "field house." Field houses are now standard among major football teams.

"There are some people that will say, 'Yeah, I saw that.' They're all lying to you. You could not foresee this in anybody."

—former Michigan right tackle Jon Jansen on the success of Tom Brady, who spent two solid but unspectacular years as Michigan's starting quarterback before going on to dominate the National Football League with the New England Patriots

GLOSSARY

All-American
Designation for players chosen as the best amateurs in the country in a particular sport.

athletic director
An administrator who oversees the coaches, players, and teams of an institution.

conference
A group of schools that join together to create a league for their sports teams.

Heisman Trophy
The award given yearly to the best player in college football.

intercollegiate
Between different colleges.

legendary
A player who is generally regarded as one of the best to ever play.

recruiting
Convincing a high school player to attend a certain college, usually to play sports.

retired
Ended one's career.

rival
An opponent with whom a player or team has a fierce and ongoing competition.

roster
A list of players who make up a team.

MORE INFORMATION

BOOKS

Mason, Tyler. *The Story of the Rose Bowl*. Minneapolis, MN: Abdo Publishing, 2016.

Wilner, Barry. *The Story of the College Football National Championship Game*. Minneapolis, MN: Abdo Publishing, 2016.

York, Andy. *Ultimate College Football Road Trip*. Minneapolis, MN: Abdo Publishing, 2019.

ONLINE RESOURCES

Booklinks
NONFICTION NETWORK
FREE! ONLINE NONFICTION RESOURCES

To learn more about the Michigan Wolverines, please visit **abdobooklinks.com** or scan this QR code. These links are routinely monitored and updated to provide the most current information available.

PLACES TO VISIT

College Football Hall of Fame

cfbhall.com

This hall of fame and museum in Atlanta, Georgia, highlights the greatest players and moments in the history of college football. Fielding Yost and Tom Harmon are among the former Wolverines enshrined here.

Michigan Stadium

mgoblue.com/sports/2017/6/16/facilities-michigan-stadium-html.aspx

Michigan Stadium has been Michigan's home field since 1927. As of 2019, the stadium, also known as "the Big House," was the largest college football stadium in the United States.

INDEX

ABOUT THE AUTHOR

Todd Ryan is a library assistant from the Upper Peninsula of Michigan. He lives near Houghton with his two cats, Izzo and Mooch.